BAR TRICKS
BAD JOKES...
AND
EVEN WORSE
STORIES

Stan Phelps and David Ackerman

Published by 9 INCH
ISBN: 978-0-9849838-8-9

DEDICATION

This book is dedicated to
John Phelps Sr. and Johnny Ackerman

TABLE OF CONTENTS

PROLOGUE

By Stan Phelps

This is a book about tricks, jokes, riddles and stories. It's been almost 20 years in the making.

By way of background, I grew up telling jokes. I owe that to my father. Somewhere along the way, I realized that the punch line to a joke was much stronger if the recipient believed it was a true story. Anchor a joke in a fragment of truth and it was exponentially funnier.

During my senior year in college, I attended a dinner for Varsity Letter athletes at Marist. The father of one of my tennis teammates attended the dinner. Jim Cagney's Dad demonstrated a trick with a napkin at our table. The trick is called "The Arb" and you'll learn about it in the Napkin tricks chapter. It was hilarious and soon I was sharing it.

I've learned the power of a funny joke, a riddle or a piece of trivia to break the ice. Humor can diffuse difficult situations. My sister Mary Ann fondly talks about the time in a hospital elevator that I broke a tense situation by sharing one of my favorite bar jokes. Here's the story:

> *I'm sitting at a bar all by myself having a drink. The bartender is standing about 30 feet away at the other end of the bar. All of sudden I hear, "Nice shirt." I look around befuddled. Am I hearing things? A couple of minutes pass and again I hear a nearby voice, "I really like your haircut." Now I'm starting to freak out. Am I hearing voices? Is*

there someone hiding behind the bar? Is the bar haunted? I get the attention of the bartender and motion her to come over. I tell her how I've heard these voices. The bartender listens attentively and then points down to a bowl of peanuts sitting on the bar. She says, "Oh, it's the nuts, they're complimentary."

After graduating from college I applied for and received a Blue Card to work in England. The program called BUNAC allowed students or recent graduates the opportunity to work for six months in Great Britain. Needing to find a flat in London, I met two recent NC State grads and we decided to share a place. In a small world scenario, Kent Lovett and Park Morris had also played college tennis. We found a place in central London. It was a one bedroom flat with three beds located in Mayfair. The apartment was on White Horse Street near Shepherd's Market just off of Piccadilly. About a week after we moved into the apartment, Park got a job two hours away up in Sheffield. Kent and I were in need of a roommate and I placed a notice on the accommodation wanted bulletin-board at the BUNAC office.

The next day I was in the apartment and the phone rang. "Hi, this is Dave. I saw your notice and wanted to know if the bed was still available." I mentioned it was and we started chatting about the program and our backgrounds. Dave mentioned he was from New York and had recently graduated from NYU. I mentioned that I had also recently graduated from a school in New York called Marist. Dave exclaimed, "Marist... we kicked their ass in tennis." We laughed and figured out that just six months earlier our teams played each other at Marist. Dave was correct as NYU trounced Marist 8-1. The sole victory for our team was mine. Buoyed by cheering crowd, I had rallied back from a 5-2 deficit in the third set against the #2 player from NYU named Trevor. Trevor was clearly the better player, but somehow I had gutted it out. After the match he laid down on the court for 10 minutes in disbelief. Dave laughed because he remembered who I was. On the two-hour ride back to Manhattan, the team teased Trevor by recalling the shouts of encouragement during our match from the home crowd, "Stan...Stan...Stan."

Two days later I took the London Underground to Kilburn to help Dave move. We became fast friends. Both Dave and Kent got jobs at a nearby bar/restaurant on Piccadilly Street named Henry's. I worked for a real estate company near Leicester Square. We had some fun times in that small apartment. One of the quirky things we did was to create a collage on our kitchen wall out of tart cards. Not familiar with tart cards, according to Wikipedia,

> Tart cards are cards advertising the services of escorts. The cards originated in the 1960s in places such as Soho, London, as handwritten postcards. As direct references to prostitution would generally be unacceptable, the cards were carefully worded and often contained euphemistic references to sex, with terms such as large chest for sale. By the late 1980s they had become black-and-white photocopied cards containing printed text and telephone numbers. In larger cities, cards began to be

placed in phone boxes. Over time they have become regarded as items of 'accidental art' and developed a cult following. They have influenced the work of mainstream  artists, inspiring collections, research, exhibitions and books.

The rules of collecting were simple. No duplicates could be posted on the wall. After a few months we had amassed a collection of over 250 cards. The sayings were kitschy and we each had our favorites. We would challenge each other to finish a saying by providing only the first word or words. Some of the sayings included, "PVC for you and me." "Roses are red, violets are blue, Christmas is coming and so may you." It was a study in design and subtle advertising copy. My favorite was one of the shorter sayings that got right to the benefit. Two words and phone number handwritten on a card, "Erections Demolished."

I share the collage story because it was a harbinger for this book coming together. Seven years after London I moved to New York City from Portland, Oregon. In a George Costanza-like moment, each day I went to Yankee Stadium to work to manage the Yankee-adidas partnership. Dave was now living in New York and managing the Blue Moon Mexican Cafe on the corner of 75th and 1st Avenue.

Over beers one night, we hatched the idea to write a book about Bar Tricks. The plan was to go out every Monday night to do research. We'd scour the city in search of tricks, jokes, riddles and interesting stories. We visited places like Chumley's. In restaurant speak, the term "86" represents "all done" or "we're out of it." Its origin dates back to the Prohibition Era in a small bar in the West Village. Still, in operation today, Chumley's is located on the corner of Bedford and Barrow. When it was a Speakeasy and customers got unruly, the owner would say, "86 Him." This meant throw them out the side door, which was 86 Bedford Street.

Over the next two years we'd collect over 100 tricks, jokes, riddles and stories. In the fall of 2000 I moved to Amsterdam. For my going away party we compiled a manuscript and created some galley copies. We had grand plans of getting the book published. Unfortunately it never happened.

Fast forward 17 years later and we are finally bringing the book to life. We hope you enjoy it as much as we enjoyed writing it.

INTRODUCTION
By David Ackerman

Dave: Hey Stan!!! Now that this whole thing is finally behind us, how did we ever get started with this book thing anyway?

Stan: Well, you being in the bar business and me, just being the natural jokester that I am, it just seemed like a great idea. Not to mention that we both like to entertain people so much. I just hope people like it.

Dave: Dude! People will definitely dig it. With all the Tricks, Riddles, Jokes and Stories, they can't go wrong. Especially since these tricks are so easy to perform, everyone will get a kick out of trying them out.

Stan: You never know, we might single handedly increase the bar business across the country.

Dave: Well, maybe we should look into getting some royalties or kickbacks?

Stan: A free drink or two would work for me Dave.

Dave: Enough said, you know being that this is our first book, I never realized how difficult this whole project would be.

Stan: You mean going out to bars every Monday night for research and talking to all of those cute waitresses. It was tough picking up all the material and a few digits too.

Dave: Not too mention all of those book meetings/dinners that we are going to expense and that whole west coast business trip to Southern California and Arizona.

Stan: 36 holes a day, that was tough!

Dave: At least the caddies gave us a trick or two. Well, regardless it sure took a while with both of our busy schedules.

Stan: Wow! I guess it wasn't easy to find time with you running a bar till all hours.

Dave: And you having to attend all those darn Yankee games for your job!

Stan: Well we did it nonetheless.

Dave: Put it there partner. (Dave and Stan shake hands)

Stan: Before we move on and let these fine people start reading the book, I'd like to clarify something... (Dave interrupts)

Dave: Seriously Stan, do you think people actually read the introduction to these books? Duh! Did you know the word gullible isn't even in the dictionary?

Stan: Whatever... I just feel like we need to clarify the difference between a bar trick and a magic trick.

Dave: Good point, clarify away...

Stan: (Stan gets up on his soap box) Well a bar trick is meant to entertain and be shared. These tricks aren't meant to fool anyone. We never show a bar trick without explaining how its done. The magic is in the sharing.

Dave & Stan: Well, that's our story and we're sticking to it. Enjoy the book!

CHAPTER 1
COIN TRICKS

"The Nines"

TYN (Things You'll Need) – Nine of the same coins (preferably pennies), a bar napkin or square coaster, an accomplice and a drink.

THE TRICK – To mysteriously pick out a coin that was touched when your back was turned.

Step 1: Set up nine coins in a tic-tac-toe format as shown Illustration 1. Take a considerable amount of time to align the coins in an exact square formation. This will act as a red herring.

Illustration 1

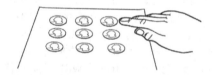

Step 2: Ask a member of the crowd to touch a coin with their fingertip while your back is turned.

Step 3: Tell your accomplice before the trick begins to set his/her drink on the corresponding corner/spot of the napkin or coaster to signal which coin was touched. For example, if the top left coin was touched as shown in Illustration 2, then the accomplice places their drink on the same corner of their napkin.

Illustration 2

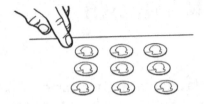

Step 4: Turn around and survey the coins. Discretely look at the drink of your accomplice, being careful not to alert anyone to the rouse. After deliberating on the nine coins and running your fingers slightly above the coins, tell the crowd which one was touched.

Step 5: Tell everyone that once you get it for the third time you'll explain the secret. After the third successful attempt, keep a straight face launch into a diatribe along these lines, "You see, everyone has oils on the tips of their fingers and the human body releases a tremendous amount of heat through its extremities. The metal in the penny, mainly the alloys in the copper react with the oils and heat. This produces a shimmer on top of the coin and a steady release of heat. You know, kind of like the sizzle on pavement during a long day in the summer sun." With this stated, ask a gullible member of the group to attempt the trick. Once he/she fails enlist the help of another member of the crowd. Pick your accomplice and watch them do the trick. You now become the accomplice and place your drink on the corresponding spot.

Enhancement 1: At some point the skeptics will start to question the trick. Most will figure there has to be some sort of communication between you and an accomplice. Tell them you understand their concerns and that once the coin has been touched, they can tell everyone to leave the room or turn their backs. Of course once your accomplice has placed their glass down, their presence is no longer necessary.

Enhancement 2: Once the trick starts to lose steam and the skeptics think there might be something fishy that only you and your accomplice can do the trick, let someone else in the group in on the trick. Tell them to put on a good show when picking the coin.

Enhancement 3: When you're feeling bold, ask a member of the group to touch two coins. This will require your accomplice to give you two signals by placing the drink on the first spot and then placing it on the second spot.. To further demonstrate your skills, ask a member of the group to place their index finger about an inch above the coins. Tell them to be careful not to actually touch the chosen coin. When you pick the coin tell the group something about heat transfer and your keen sense of thermodynamics.

"Mother of All Coin Tricks"

TYN (Things You'll Need) – Three coins: a penny, a nickel and a quarter.

THE TRICK – To see who is the last person in the group to figure out whom the third coin is.

Step 1: Spread out the three coins in the following order: Penny, Nickel and Quarter.

Step 2: Tell everyone to observe the coins. While they are observing, point at the coins while posing the following question: "Tommy's Mother has three kids... Penny (point at the penny), Nicole (point at the nickel), and _____? Point at the quarter and ask, 'Who is the third?'"

Step 3: Tell everyone that you are going to let each person take a guess. Alert them that it's not as important to find out who the third child is, because everyone will eventually get it. Rather this is a game to see whom the last person is to find out. Tell everyone that if the answer becomes obvious, don't blurt it out. Have them come over and whisper it as not to ruin the game for the rest of the group. Now have everyone take a guess. Almost always, no one will guess correctly on the first round.

Step 4: Repeat the question while pointing at the coins. Remind everyone not to blurt out the answer if they get it. Ask everyone to take a guess. 90% of the time people will not guess the correct answer, mostly because they are looking at the coins and not listening to the question.

Step 5: Repeat until the last person gets the correct answer. Stress Tommy or cover the coins with your hand while asking the question if you need to give clues. It's fun to tell people that there is a life lesson in this trick: "In life, people always look, they never listen. That's why a picture is worth a thousand words."

"Getting it Straight"

TYN – Four of the same coins, preferably quarters

THE TRICK – Set up four quarters into a straight line in four moves.

Step 1: Arrange the quarters as shown in Illustration 1.

Illustration 1

Step 2: Instruct the group that they will be allowed four moves and that each move consists of one quarter at a time. For a move to be valid, the moving quarter must be touching the edges of two other quarters. No pushing of the coins or placing them on top of one another.

Step 3: If the group is unable to solve the trick, demonstrate how it's done by moving the quarters as shown in Illustrations 2-5.

Illustration 2

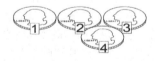

Illustration 3

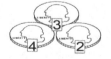

Illustration 4

Illustration 5

"Dime for Every Quarter"

TYN (Things You'll Need) – A crisp dollar bill and ten quarters.

THE TRICK – Tell someone that you'll give them a dime for every quarter they can stand on edge as long as they balance a total of ten.

Step 1: Throw down the challenge. Demonstrate how easy it is by balancing a coin on its edge.

Step 2: Patiently watch as your challenger balances the 10 quarters.

Step 3: Act gracious as you hand out a crisp dollar to your opponent. Then quickly gather all ten of their quarters and place them in your pocket. Be sure to say "thanks" as you're now $1.50 richer.

Story: Origin of "On the Wagon"

In the days of the Old West, they used to give prisoners their last drink before they were to be hung. They were carted down to the saloon. After having a drink, they would be approached by the bartender who would ask, "Care for another?" At that point, the jailer would step forward and declare: "He or she can't – they are ON THE WAGON."

JOKE: Mushroom walks into a bar...

He orders a beer. Bartender says, "I'm sorry, we don't serve your kind here." The mushroom exclaims, "Why not, I'm a Fun-Guy."

"SPOOF"

TYN – A Minimum of four participants and two coins (any coins) per participant.

THE TRICK – A fun group guessing game of elimination.

Step 1: Instruct everyone that they are to have two coins. During each round, they will each place either zero, one or two coins in their right hand.

Step 2: Once everyone has held their right fist forward, each member of the group will guess the total number of coins everyone is holding. Each person will take a guess in a clockwise order starting with the person who introduced the trick. Each of the guesses must be a different number.

Step 3: After everyone has guessed, each person opens their hand and the coins are counted. The person who guessed correctly is out of the game. The process is then repeated as the person sitting to the left of the person who guessed correctly in the previous round starts the guessing.

Step 4: Report the process until you are left with two participants. This will be the final round determining the losing member of the group.

Enhancement – To create additional buzz around the game it is fun to come up with some stakes for those participants who finish last and second to last. For example, the person who finishes last buys a round of drinks for the group. It is also fun to see if you can raise the stakes when it gets down to the final two participants. Encourage them to create a side-bet to sweeten the pot.

"Snatch"

TYN – One coin, preferably a quarter.

THE TRICK – Be able to snatch a coin out of someone's hand before they can close it.

Step 1: Place the coin directly into the center of the open left palm of your subject. Place their palm in front of them, facing up, just above waist level as shown in Illustration 1.

Illustration 1

Step 2: Stand facing your subject and raise your right hand about 18 inches above the open palm.

Step 3: Instruct your subject to close their hand once you attempt to snatch the quarter.

Step 4: Snatch the quarter by brushing across the fingers of the subject open hand as shown in Illustration 2. The slight contact will cause the quarter to jump an inch. As you continue to brush across the hand, grab the quarter. With a little practice you should be able to snatch quarters from even the quickest of subjects.

Illustration 2

Enhancement: Once you've mastered the snatch trick, consider adding the following nuance to the trick. Take a penny or a dime and conceal it by holding it by its edge between the crease at the base of your fingers/hand. Then hold your hand like a claw over the hand of your subject, thumb and four fingers pointing down. Tell them you are going to grab their quarter before they can close their hand. As you descend on your subject, let go of the penny or dime and strike the open palm with your thumb and four fingers extended. Like the brush, this will cause the quarter to jump. Close your fingers and grab the quarter. If you execute the trick successfully, the subject will have closed their hand

and think they have retained the coin, only to find a dime or penny. While they are showing you their coin, pocket the quarter discreetly and then display an empty hand. The quarter has turned into a dime.

Story: What does karaoke mean?

Karaoke is Japanese for "ear pain." Actually it means, "without an orchestra."

Riddle: What is it?

Arnold Schwarzenegger has a big one...
Michael J. Fox has a little one...
Madonna doesn't have one...
The Pope has one but doesn't use it...
Bill Clinton uses his all the time...
Jerry Seinfeld is quite proud of his...
George Burns' was hot...
And you never saw Lucy use Desi's

What is it? **Answer:** Page 93

CHAPTER 2
HAND TRICKS

"Contortion 101"

TYN (Things You'll Need) – Two hands.

THE TRICK – Challenge everyone to perform a basic contortionist move using two hands.

Step 1: Have each person extend their left hand directly out in front of them. Tell them to point their left thumb towards the floor. Demonstrate yourself as shown in Illustration 1.

Illustration 1

Step 2: Tell everyone to take their right hand and place it over their left had. The thumb in your right hand should be pointing towards the floor. Have everyone clasp their hands and interlock their fingers as shown in Illustration 2.

Illustration 2

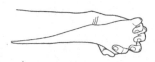

Step 3: Release your hands and tell everyone that their hands need to be held a little higher. Help one or two participants to raise their hands slightly.

While everyone is adjusting, place your hands together near your waist in a praying fashion as seen in Illustration 3. Twist your right wrist counter clockwise 180 degrees to make your hands resemble the rest of the group as seen in Illustration 4. Raise your hand up to the level near everyone else.

Illustration 3

Illustration 4

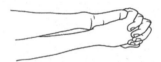

Step 4: Now the contortion begins. Tell everyone to lift their hands up towards their head while bending their elbows and pushing their palms out. Then demonstrate the move finishing as shown in Illustration 5. No one else in the group will be able to execute the move.

Illustration 5

Step 5: As a rouse, tell everyone that you will reveal the key to the trick. Share that the key is having your thumbs interlocked. Again, have everyone place their left thumb down and then their right hand over with fingers interlocked. Release your hands as you tell everyone that you will need to check their thumbs. Reassure the group that you think they have the correct thumb positioning. While everyone is focusing on their thumbs, repeat the process of arranging your hands in a praying fashion near your waist as shown in Illustration 3. Demonstrate the solution like before (Illustration 4 and 5) and challenge the group to do the same.

Step 6: Repeat the process till everyone gets thoroughly frustrated and then demonstrate the slight of hand.

"A Nose that Always Knows"

TYN – Two hands and a nose.

THE TRICK – To perform a simple hand trick that will stump your friends.

Step 1: Similar to the previous trick, you will ask each member of the group to place their left hand out in front of them with their thumb pointing down. Have them place their right hand over their left and interlock their fingers as shown in Illustration 1. You will also assume the position being careful to covertly place your right pinky finger over your left pinky finger when you interlock your fingers.

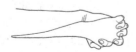

Step 2: While you demonstrate, tell everyone to bring their hands under their chin as shown in Illustration 2. Tell them to extend their pointing fingers while keeping them crossed, placing their pointing fingers on each side of their nose.

Step 3: Once everyone has their pointing fingers in place – tell them to release their hands while keeping their pointing fingers on their nose. While they struggle – demonstrate the solution and rub it in by wiggling your fingers. Usually one or two out of 10 in the group will be able to perform the feat.

Step 4: Repeat the process a couple of times until everyone is thoroughly frustrated. Then be kind and show the solution.

Joke: Did you hear about the alcoholic dyslexic? He walked into a bra!

Bonus dyslexic jokes:

Did you hear about the evil dyslexic? He's the one that sold his soul to Santa.

Did you hear about the dyslexic insomniac that was agnostic? He's the one who stays up all night wondering if there is such thing as a dog.

Story: The Origin of Cheers and Clanking glasses.

The tradition of raising your glass, touching glasses with friends and saying "Cheers" before drinking, dates back to medieval days when kings and knights thought their drinks might be poisoned. In order to be sure, they weren't drinking poison, they would fiercely clank their glasses in the hopes of splashing the poisoned drinks into everyone else's.

"Liquid Handcuffs"

TYN – An unsuspecting victim and one pint of beer.

THE TRICK – To immobilize your unsuspecting victim at the bar using just one pint of beer.

Step 1: Ask the person that you'll be doing this gag on to place his or her thumbs on the bar counter with the rest of their hands below the bar as shown in Illustration 1.

Illustration 1

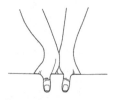

Step 2: Make sure the person's thumbs are about an inch apart. Then take the full pint of beer and quickly place it on their thumbs as shown in Illustration 2.

Illustration 2

Step 3: Ask your volunteer to now try to escape without spilling a drop of beer. Try as they may it is impossible to escape the liquid handcuffs.

Step 4: After your victim has suffered enough and everyone's had their laugh, wait five more minutes and then put them out of their misery.

Enhancement: Bet anyone a beer that they can't drink a pint without their two thumbs, they can touch the glass but they can't use their two thumbs. Tell them they must place their thumbs on the bar and that they can only touch the pint once you've placed it down.

CHAPTER 3
NAPKIN TRICKS

"The Ultimate Wedding Trick"

TYN (Things You'll Need) – A linen napkin with seams and five toothpicks.

THE TRICK – Astonish your friends by placing a perfectly good toothpick inside a folded up napkin in your hand. After a volunteer feels around and finds the toothpick, ask them to snap it. Then open the napkin to present the same perfectly good toothpick.

Step 1: Covertly get five toothpicks. Discretely place one toothpick into each of the four corners of the napkin. Be careful to thread them into the seams to insure they are not visible. Place the remaining toothpick on the table.

Step 2: Announce to everyone that you have an interesting trick with a napkin and a toothpick. Show the fifth toothpick and then take the napkin and raise it up outstretched by its corners. Show everyone the front and back so nobody expects foul play.

Step 3: Place the open napkin on your left palm facing up as shown in Illustration 1. Then ask someone to pick up the toothpick, examine it and place it in the middle of the napkin.

Illustration 1

Step 4: Proceed to fold each of the corners of the napkin into the middle. While you are folding, cup the napkin with your left hand to cover the toothpick by making a fist. This will insure it does not get broken. Use your right hand to hold all of the corners snugly into the middle.

Step 5: Ask your volunteer to feel around in the napkin while it's still in your hand. Their task is to feel around for the toothpick and to announce when they've found it. They will eventually locate one of the toothpicks that are in the seams of the napkin. Once they've located the toothpick, ask them to break it. If it's quiet enough, everyone should be able to hear it actually snap.

Step 6: Now place the napkin on the table and slowly unfold it until you get to the last remaining fold that conceals the original toothpick. Very carefully uncover the final fold revealing the perfectly good toothpick. You have three other toothpicks in the seams, you'll be able do the trick a few more times.

Enhancement: For added effect, you can blow on the napkin or wiggle your fingers over the napkin while chanting something unrecognizable. As you slowly and deliberately unfold the napkin with a look of amazement as you reveal the original toothpick unscathed.

"The ARB"

TYN – One napkin per person, preferably cloth or linen.

THE TRICK – Have everyone fold their napkins in a certain way, then pull at the corners to mimic wearing a bra.

Step 1: Tell everyone to place their napkin on their lap or on top of the table as shown in Illustration 1.

Illustration 1

Step 2: Instruct everyone to fold the top into the middle and the bottom into the middle as shown in Illustration 2.

Illustration 2

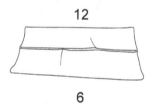

Step 3: Demonstrate picking up the napkin by pinching and picking the napkin up at 12 o'clock and six o'clock. Once everyone has correctly picked up their napkin, tell them to place it back down on the table as shown in Illustration 3.

Illustration 3

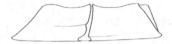

Step 4: Pinch the top corners between your thumb and pointing finger. Then instruct everyone to find the bottom corners and pinch them with the top corners as shown in Illustration 4. Check to insure that everyone has pinched the corners correctly.

Illustration 4

Step 5: Instruct everyone to hold both hands under their chin as shown in Illustration 5. Tell everyone on the count of 3 to pull the corners to their armpits. One, two, three and everyone pulls, revealing a pseudo bra as shown in Illustration 6.

Illustration 5   **Illustration 6**

Enhancement: Have half of the group place the napkin on the top of their head, instead of underneath their chin. Tell them to pull each hand to their ears. You now have a jester hat or animal ears.

Riddle: Half of all Americans

One half of all Americans live within 50 miles of what? **Answer:** Page 93

Riddle: Water

A guy walks into a bar and orders a glass of water. All of a sudden, the bartender pulls a gun out from behind the bar and points it at the customer. Startled, the guy steps back and says, "Thanks, I appreciate that, I don't need the water anymore." Why did he want the water in the first place? **Answer:** Page

Joke: Did you hear about the guy who walked into a bar? He said "Ouch!"

Bonus Joke: Did you hear about the two guys that walked into a bar? You'd think the second one would have ducked.

Story: Where does Gin & Tonic come from?
Gin and Tonic takes its origin from the British Navy. At sea the sailors were given quinine to treat malaria and limes to prevent scurvy. They were also given a daily ration of gin or rum to keep them in line. The sailors would combine all three to take their medicine.

Story: Where does IPA come from?
The type of beer IPA stands for India Pale Ale. It owes its origin to the British Army. Soldiers as part

of their salary were rationed an amount of beer each week. When soldiers served in India the Army was faced with a dilemma. Beer shipped from England would be spoiled by the time it reached New Delhi. The solution was to load the beer up with hops. Hops are a natural preservative and give an IPA its distinctive taste.

"A rose, is a rose, is a . . ."

TYN - A bar napkin.

TRICK – Make a rose (albeit a paper one) out of a bar napkin.

Step 1: Unfold the napkin and fold it around your pointing finger and index finger as shown in Illustration 1.

Illustration 1

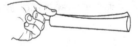

Step 2: About two inches below the napkin, start to twist the napkin tightly to the bottom of the napkin as shown in Illustration 2.

Illustration 2

Step 3: Tweak the opening to make the napkin resemble the opening of the rose. Search the room

and give your creation away. You'll make someone's day.

Enhancements: You can improve upon your rose by adding a leaf. About halfway through twisting the napkin tightly, rip a small piece off of the napkin and continue twisting to the bottom.

Riddle: Two Identical Twins

Two identical twins walk into a bar. They both order a scotch on the rocks. One gulps it while the other drinks it slowly. The one that drinks it slowly dies. Why? (Clue: Why would you die if you if you drank something?) **Answer:** Page 93

"Cork in a bottle"

TYN – An empty wine bottle, a cork and a linen napkin.

THE TRICK – Retrieve a cork out of a wine bottle by using a napkin.

Step 1: Push the cork through the neck of the bottle.

Step 2: Challenge your friends to retrieve the cork out of the bottle by only using the napkin and their hands.

Step 3: After your friends struggle miserably show them the solution. This is done by taking the napkin and folding it as shown in Illustration 1.

Illustration 1

Step 4: Take the napkin and insert it through the stem of the wine bottle. Proceed to tilt the bottle until the cork falls into the opening as shown in Illustration 2.

Illustration 2

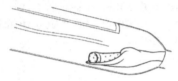

Step 5: Once the cork is securely in the opening, pull the napkin out of the bottle. The cork will follow.

Joke: A termite walks into a bar.

He asks the waitress, "Is the bar–tender here?"

CHAPTER 4
BOTTLE TRICKS

"Pull the Rug Out, Part 1"

TYN (Things You'll Need) – An empty beer bottle, a dollar bill and two quarters.

THE TRICK – Swiftly whisk a dollar bill off a bottle that has two quarters balanced on it.

Step 1: Set up the bottle, two quarters and dollar bill as shown in Illustration 1. Challenge your friends to attempt to remove the bill from the bottle without dropping the quarter. Instruct them that they are not allowed to touch the quarters, only the bill.

Illustration 1

Step 2: After they fail to solve the trick, show them the solution. As you set up the trick the quarters should be slightly balanced to the left to corner as shown in Illustration 2.

Illustration 2

Step 3: With one swift and decisive motion extend your pointing and middle finger out and slap down on the right portion of the bill. The coins should stay on the bottle while the bill slides from underneath.

Enhancements – It helps if you lick your fingers prior to slapping them down on the dollar. You'll find yourself a lot more successful if you aim just right of the bottle and not the end of the bill.

"Pull the Rug Out – Part Deux"

TYN – A dollar bill and an empty beer bottle.

THE TRICK – To successfully pull out a dollar bill from underneath an upside down empty beer bottle without touching the bottle with your hands.

Step 1: Set up the dollar bill and beer bottle as shown in Illustration 1. Challenge everyone to attempt to remove the bill without tipping the bottle. Instruct them that they are only able to touch the dollar bill and not the bottle.

Illustration 1

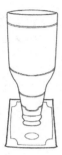

Step 2: Very few if any will be able to snatch the dollar bill without tipping the bottle. The easiest way to perform this trick is to start rolling the bill slowly towards the bottle as shown in Illustration 2.

Illustration 2

Step 3: Once you've rolled the bill up to the bottle, continue rolling slowly until the bill slides completely from underneath.

"Squeeze Play"

TYN – A peeled hard boiled egg, an empty bottle, a napkin and matches.

THE TRICK – To get a hard boiled egg through the small opening of a bottle without using your hands.

Step 1: Find a bottle that has an opening big enough to fit one-third of the egg in as shown in Illustration 1. A Snapple bottle works well.

Illustration 1

Step 2: Light a small piece of paper/napkin on fire and drop it into the bottle.

Step 3: Place the egg on top of the bottle. As the flame expends the oxygen in the bottle, suction will be created and the egg will get squeezed into the bottle.

"Snap, Crackle, & Pop"

TYN – An empty plastic water bottle, preferably ribbed.

THE TRICK – To make an unsuspecting group think that you are "big time" cracking your neck.

Step 1: Take the empty bottle without the cap and covertly place it behind your neck, about halfway down your collar.

Step 2: Grab the top part of the bottle in hand and place your other hand under your chin.

Step 3: Draw attention to the fact that your neck is bothering you. While everyone noticing you tilting your head with your hand to the left and right, announce that you usually crack your neck to remedy the situation. Then simulate that you are wrenching your neck as you squeeze the bottle. The loud cracking noise will cause concern among your group as the others shudder in reaction to your prank.

Enhancements: A great trick on the golf course.

Joke: What's the difference between beer nuts and deer nuts?

Beer nuts are a $1.49 and deer nuts are under a buck.

CHAPTER 5
GLASS TRICKS

"Finger & Thumb"

TYN (Things You'll Need) - A wine glass and two dimes.

THE TRICK – Grab two dimes which are balanced on opposite ends of a wine glass using only your thumb and index finder.

Step 1: Set up the trick by placing the two dimes on opposite ends of the rim of the wine glass as shown in Illustration 1. Begin by pinching them against the glass with you thumb and index finger as shown in Illustration 2.

Illustration 1   **Illustration 2**

Step 2: Most people will slide the dimes horizontally towards each other. This makes it almost impossible to grab without dropping the dimes. The solution requires the dimes to be slid vertically down to the stem of the glass as shown in Illustration 3.

Illustration 3

Step 3: Once you've reached the stem, simply touch the coins together and pull away from the glass.

"The Disappearing Quarter"

TYN – A quarter, three white paper bar napkins and a tumbler/rocks glass.

THE TRICK – Make a quarter disappear right in front of your eyes.

Step 1: Before you attempt this trick, a little set up is required. First you'll need to attach a bar napkin to the opening of a glass as shown in Illustration 1. Do this by unfolding the bar napkin once so it has two plies and lay it down on the bar.

Illustration 1

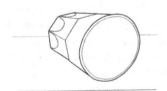

Step 2: Now moisten the rim of the glass and press it firmly down on the napkin. Tear away the parts of the napkin that are outside of the glass as shown in Illustration 2. This set up should not be performed in front of the group, as it would ruin the trick.

Illustration 2

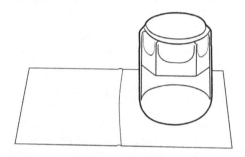

Step 3: Take another bar napkin, unfold it once and lay it on the bar. Now place a quarter on the left hand side and the tumbler glass on the right as shown in Illustration 3. No one should suspect anything, as the napkin covering the mouth of the glass should blend with the napkin on the bar. You are now ready to perform the trick.

Illustration 3

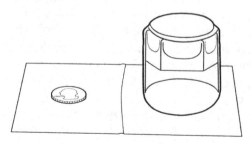

Step 4: Announce to the group that you will be able to make the quarter disappear right in front of their eyes. Take the third bar napkin and unfold it completely and cover the tumbler glass as shown in Illustration 4.

Illustration 4

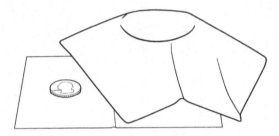

Step 5: Now grab the covered glass and move it to the left to cover the quarter. Chant a few unrecognizable words and uncover the napkin. To everyone's amazement, the quarter seems to have vanished as it sits underneath the glass.

Joke: I'll have a 15.

A new bartender is training at the local bar. A brunette walks in on his first day and asks for a B.L. Perplexed, he shares that he doesn't know what a BL is. The customer says, "Bud Light DUH!" The next day a redhead asks for a V&T. The bartender apologizes for not knowing. The customer says, "Vodka and tonic... DUH!" On his third day a blond approaches the bar and asks for a 15. The bartender thought he knew it all at this point but is still clueless. He apologizes and asks what a fifteen is. The customer chuckles and says, "15!.. 7&7 DUH!"

Riddle: Greater Than God

What's greater than God?
More evil than the devil,
The rich want for it,
The poor have it,
And if you eat it... you will die.

What is it?

CLUES:
1.   Take each saying individually
2.   A higher percentage of second graders compared to members of MENSA (160 IQ+) get this correct. **Answer:** Page 93

"The Vacuum"

TYN – An ashtray, a dime, an olive, a matchbook, a shot glass and water.

THE TRICK – Pick a dime out of a water filled ashtray without getting your fingers wet.

Step 1: Setup the trick by placing a dime in an ashtray and placing a small amount of water to cover the dime as shown in Illustration 1. Notice that the dime is placed near the edge of the ashtray. Challenge the audience to solve the trick by utilizing the following items: an olive, a book of matches and a shot glass. Instruct them that they are only allowed to touch the dime with their fingers. If their fingers get wet, they've lost the trick.

Illustration 1

Step 2: Allow your audience to attempt to solve the trick. Once they've given up, demonstrate the solution. Take the olive and stick two matches into curved end as shown in Illustration 2.

Illustration 2

Step 3: Place the olive in the ashtray at least two inches from inches from the dime. Light the two matches and then quickly place the shot glass over the olive and the matches as shown in Illustration 3.

Illustration 3

Step 4: As the matches expend the oxygen in the glass, a vacuum effect will be created. It will create suction and draw the water from the ashtray into the glass. You will now be able to take the dime out of the ashtray without getting your fingers wet.

"Waterworld / Waterfalls"

TYN – Two identical glasses (pint, wine or rocks) filled with water and a dime.
THE TRICK – Place a dime into two glasses on top of one another and filled with water without spilling a drop.

Step 1: First you'll need to set up the glasses and the water. This can be done two different ways. One way is to submerge both glasses into a sink or bucket filled with water, placing the rims of the glasses together under the water. Another way is to fill both glasses up with water. Then you take a cardboard bar coaster and place it on top of one of the glasses. You then turn the glasses with the coaster upside down and place it on the other glass. Now slide the coaster carefully out, leaving just the two full glasses. The end effect of either option is shown in Illustration 1.

Illustration 1

Step 2: Challenge everyone to attempt the trick. Instruct them they are not allowed to touch either of the glasses with any part of their body.

Step 3: To solve the trick, you must tap the top glass gently with the dime. This tapping will cause the top glass to move slightly to create an opening. Once the opening is big enough for the dime, slide it in and no water will be spilled.

Enhancement: Once you've demonstrated the trick, challenge the group to get all of the water out of the top glass without being able to touch the glass with anything. With a towel ready, demonstrate the solution. All you have to do is blow at the opening where you slid the dime in and all the water will spill out.

"Beer Drinking Contest"

TYN – Three pints of beer and three shots of beer.

THE TRICK – To be able to drink three pints of beer before your opponent can down three small shot glasses of beer.

Step 1: Find a willing opponent that will join you in the contest. Instruct your opponent that there are two rules of the game. First, they can't touch their first shot glass until you finish your first pint and place it down. Second, they can't touch any of your pint glasses.

Step 2: Set out three pints in front of you and three shot glasses in front of your opponent. Start out on your first pint (take your time as there's no rush).

When you finish it, turn it upside down and cover one of the shots of beer as shown in Illustration 1.

Illustration 1

Step 3: Your opponent is stuck since he/she can't touch any of your pint glasses as stated in the rules.

Joke: Ham sandwich walks into a bar...

A ham sandwich walks into a bar and orders a beer. The bartender takes one look at him and says, "Sorry, we don't serve food here."

"The Egg Jump"

TYN – Two shot glasses and a raw egg.

THE TRICK – Jump an egg from one shot glass to another without physically touching the egg or the glass.

Step 1: Set up the egg and the glasses as shown in Illustration 1. Challenge everyone to attempt to solve the trick.

Illustration 1

Step 2: To demonstrate the solution, get eye-level with the glasses and blow real hard and quick onto the top portion of the egg. The egg will jump over into the second shot glass.

Story: Origin of "the whole nine yards?"

Where does the term "the whole nine yards" come from? According to the New York Times, the answer to the question has been the "Bigfoot of word origins, chased around wild speculative corners by amateur word freaks, with exasperated lexicographers and debunkers of folk etymologies in hot pursuit." My favorite explanation is that the phrase came from W.W.II fighter pilots in the South Pacific. While arming their airplanes on the ground, the .50 caliber machine gun ammo belts measured exactly 27 feet before being loaded into the fuselage. If the pilots fired all of their ammo at a target, the enemy got "the whole nine yards."

"Leaning Tower of Cerveza"

TYN – A pint of beer, a wooden match and a bar napkin.

THE TRICK – Balance a pint of beer on its edge.

Step 1: Covertly take a wooden match and place under a bar napkin. Take a full pint and balance it as shown in Illustration 1.

Illustration 1

Step 2: Challenge your friends to do the same.

Riddle: 14th Floor

Charlie owns a bar on the 14th floor of a building in midtown. Everyday Charlie closes the bar, takes the elevator down to the ground floor and walks home. Every morning he walks to work, takes the elevator to the 12th floor, has to get out and walk the remaining two flights of stairs. The only time he takes the elevator all the way up to the 14th floor is either: 1. If someone is in the elevator with him, or 2. If it is raining outside. Why does he have to get off at the 12th floor? **Answer:** Page 93

"Shootin' Glass"

TYN – Two empty pint glasses.

THE TRICK – How to separate two stacked pint glasses without physically touching them.

41

Step 1: Place one pint glass into the other. Lay them down on the counter as shown in Illustration 1.

Illustration 1

Step 2: The trick is solved by blowing into the top opening between the two glasses as shown in Illustration 2.

Illustration 2

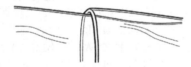

Riddle: Joe and Fred

You're the investigator. You notice on your way home at 5:00 a.m. that the door to the local dive beach/hangout called Under the Sea is ajar. You investigate and walk into the bar. You notice that the back window is open and that there is water and broken glass on the floor. You realize that Joe & Fred are dead. Who are Joe and Fred? **Answer:** Page 93

"Lasso the Ice"

TYN – A full glass of water with ice, a six inch piece of string and a pinch of salt.

THE TRICK – Pick up a cube of ice from a glass of ice water with a string without touching the ice or the glass with your hands.

Step 1: Lay a piece of string or dental floss across the top of the glass as shown in Illustration 1. A portion of the string should be lying across the cube.

Illustration 1

Step 2: Pour some salt on the portion of the string that's resting on the cube. The salt will cause the ice to temporarily melt and then refreeze.

Step 3: Gently pick up each end of the string, lifting the cube out of the glass of water as shown in Illustration 2.

Illustration 2

Joke: A fish walks into a bar.

The bartender says: "What'll you have?" (In a raspy voice) The fish says, "W A – T E R"

Joke: Horse walks into bar

The bartender takes one look at him and says, "Why such a long face?"

"Balancing Act – Part One / The Shot Glass"

TYN – A bill ($1, $5, $10 or $20), two pint glasses and a shot glass.

THE TRICK – To balance a shot glass on a bill between two upside down pint glasses.

Step 1: Set two pint glasses upside down about two inches apart at their base as shown in Illustration 1. Hand the bill to the group and challenge them to balance the shot glass between the two glasses using only the bill for support.

Illustration 1

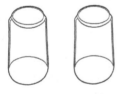

Step 2: Demonstrate the solution by corrugating the bill as shown in Illustration 2. This is done by

making small quarter inch folds lengthwise throughout the bill.

Illustration 2

Step 3: Place the bill on top of the two glasses and then balance the shot glass as shown in Illustration 3.

Illustration 3

"Coaster Suction"

TYN – A full pint of beer and a coaster.

THE TRICK – To hold a pint of beer upside down with the aid of a coaster without spilling a drop.

Step 1: Place a coaster on top of a full pint of beer as shown in Illustration 1.

Illustration 1

Step 2: Hold the coaster in place while you turn the pint upside down as shown in Illustration 2.

Illustration 2

Step 3: Let go of the coaster and to your friend's amazement it remains. The simple concept of suction holds it in place.

Story: Origin of a Screwdriver

Why is Vodka and orange juice called a Screwdriver?

The mixture was popularized by workers in the oil fields who used their tools, namely a screwdriver to stir up the drink.

CHAPTER 6
CONDIMENT TRICKS

"Sugar/Sweet & Low"

TYN - Three packets of sugar and two packets of Sweet & Low per participant.

The Trick - To challenge the group to create separation between three sugars and two Sweet & Low packets in five moves as shown from Illustration 1 to Illustration 2.

Step 1: Place the five packets in the order as shown in Illustration 1. Instruct the group that the goal is to have all of the Sweet & Low packets on one side and all of sugars on the other side in five moves.

Explain the Rules:

1. You must move one sugar and one Sweet & Low at a time. They must be next to each other for a move to be valid.
2. Moving one or two of the same is prohibited.
3. You are not allowed to scrunch/move together the packets after a move.

Illustration 1

Illustration 2

Step 2: Explain to everyone that you will demonstrate the solution to give them a head start. Quickly go through the moves in Illustrations 3 to 7 and then ask them to attempt the solution.

Illustration 3

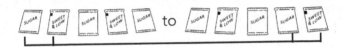

Illustration 4

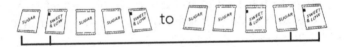

Illustration 5

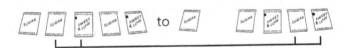

Illustration 6

Illustration 7

Step 3: Keep demonstrating the solution until everyone gets the trick.

Riddle: Spoiler

What is the only food that doesn't spoil? **Answer:** Page 93

"Magic Pepper"

TYN - Pepper shaker and 2-4 participants.

The Trick - To make it seem like a sprinkle of pepper magically goes from the top hand to the bottom hand.

Set up: Covertly wet the tip of your finger and press it down into some pepper that you secretly sprinkled onto the table.

Step 1: Ask your participants to extend both of their arms forward and palms facing down to the ground.

Step 2: Secretly transfer the pepper from the tip of your finger to the open palm of one of the participants. This is done by telling everyone to raise his or her hands higher. Press the tip of your finger on one of the outstretched palms as an effort to raise the hands of the person whose are the lowest. To divert their attention from your finger, you might want to grab their other wrist with your other hand.

Step 3: Now ask everyone to make a fist with each hand. Arrange their fists one on top of the other. Be careful to place the hand with the pepper in it at the bottom.

Step 4: Take the peppershaker and sprinkle a tiny bit of pepper on the top hand. Tell everyone that you are attempting to send the pepper through everyone's hands into the bottom. Ask for their complete concentration, chant a few words and then smack down on the top hand so that the pepper flies.

Step 5: Now start opening and inspecting each hand starting from the top. As you get to the last couple of hands, use a little showmanship to inspect and brush each hand looking for pepper. When you get to the last hand, have your subject slowly open it. The magic pepper is revealed.

Joke: Dat's my Simon

Three women from the Caribbean are in a bar talking about their boyfriends. They are comparing them to drinks. The first speaks up and says, "If my boyfriend Michael was a drink, he'd be a 7 UP. Because he's seven inches and he's always up. The second woman interjects, "Dat ain't a ting. If my Christopher was a drink, he'd be a Mountain Dew. Because he mounts me, then he do's me. Not to be outdone, the last one exclaims, "If my Simon was a drink, he'd be a Jack Daniels." After a couple of seconds of silence, her girlfriends retort, "Jack Daniels, girl! Dat's a hard liquor." Quickly she responds, "Dat's my Simon."

"Balancing Act – Part Deux"

TYN - An egg and some salt.

The Trick - Defy the laws of gravity by balancing an egg on its tip.

Set up - Covertly pour a small mound of salt on the bar counter.

Step 1: Balance the egg on its tip using the small mound of salt as shown in Illustration 1.

Illustration 1

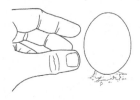

Step 2: Now covertly blow away the excess salt and call attention to your feat. Challenge others to do the same.

Riddle: Hangman

You walk into an empty bar with no tables and chairs. A man has hung himself from a ceiling fan in the middle of the room. His feet dangle five feet above the ground. The only thing on the floor is four inches of water.

How did he get up that high to hang himself?
Answer: Page 93

CHAPTER 7
DOLLAR TRICKS

"You Catch It – You Keep It"

TYN (Things You'll Need) - A dollar bill.

The Trick - Catch a dollar between your fingers as someone drops it from close range.

Step 1: Find a volunteer and challenge him/her to attempt to catch a dropped dollar bill. Instruct them that if they can catch it, they can keep it.

Step 2: Hold a dollar bill vertically and ask your volunteer to place their thumb and four fingers on either side of the bill as shown in Illustration 1. Their fingers should be slightly above the face on the bill.

Illustration 1

Step 3: Drop the bill and watch as your volunteer misses the bill again and again.

Story: The origin of the word "Buck"

Back in the frontier days, traders and trappers would barter for supplies. Pelts and buckskins were the major form of currency. Bucks became the slang. The saying "pass the buck' was immortalized by Harry S Truman. He had a plaque of his White House desk that read, "The buck stops here."

Riddle: Three Statements

What am I describing by the following three statements?

1. He/She who makes it, sells it.
2. He/She who buys it, doesn't use it.
3. And, he/she who uses it, doesn't realize he/she is using it.

Clue: Concentrate on the third statement. Why would someone not realize that they are using something? **Answer:** Page 93

"Magnetic Dollar"

TYN - a dollar bill and a cigarette.

The Trick - To take an ordinary dollar bill and demonstrate its magnetic qualities.

Step 1: Take a dollar bill and fold it in half. Place it between your fingers as shown in Illustration 1.

Illustration 1

Step 2: Then place the cigarette on the table. Drag the cigarette in a pulling motion. As you drag, keep your mouth slightly open and then slightly start blowing towards the cigarette. With a little practice, you should be able to roll the cigarette towards the dollar.

Step 3: Let everyone give it a try. After a few of their unsuccessful attempts, explain that you possess animal magnetism and then demonstrate the trick again.

Riddle: Dead Presidents

Can you name the Presidents on the one, five and ten dollar bills? **Answer:** Page 93

"Five On Fire"

TYN: A book of matches and a glass of brandy.

The Trick: Bet someone a beer that you can set his/her five dollar bill on fire and then pay for your beer with it.

Step 1: Thoroughly soak the five dollar bill in the brandy. Make sure the bill is soaked well as show in Illustration 1.

Illustration 1

Step 2: Light the bill on fire. Only the brandy will burn as shown in Illustration 2.

Illustration 2

Step 3: Blow out the flames once the brandy is burnt. This way the flames won't burn the bill.

Step 4: Now pay for your drink with the five dollar bill you just won.

Story: Three Sheets to the Wind

This phrase came about from watchmen on sailboats. Each sailboat has three sails. The job of the watchmen was to make sure the sails didn't get tangled in the wind. Occasionally one sail would get all twisted and knotted. This would be trouble, especially if the watchmen didn't see what was happening. If the watchmen happened to be sleeping or drunk, he/she might miss that all three sails getting tangled. Thus, they were "three sheets to the wind."

CHAPTER 8
STRAW TRICKS

"Beer Snorkel"

TYN (Things You'll Need) – A full bottle of beer, a straw and a pack of matches.

THE TRICK – To shotgun a bottle of beer using only a straw.

Step 1: Take a drinking straw and bend it with the heat of a match to a 45-degree angle. Once the straw is bent, make sure you still have suction and the ability for air to travel within the straw.

Step 2: Place the long end of the straw in the bottle. Put the opening of the bottle to your mouth with the straw hanging to the side.

Step 3: Tilt the bottle back, open your throat, and guzzle – guzzle – guzzle. The straw allows air into the bottle, gravity takes care of the rest.

Riddle: All 50 States

Challenge someone if they can say all 50 states in less than 15 seconds. **Answer:** Page 93

"Raising a Bottle"

TYN – An empty beer bottle and a straw.

THE TRICK – Pick up an empty beer bottle using only a straw.

Step 1: Bend the straw and place it in the bottle as shown Illustration 1.

Illustration 1

Step 2: As soon as you feel the bend open up just past the throat of the bottle, lift the straw up and the bottle will follow as shown in Illustration 2.

Illustration 2

Joke: Taxi Cab

A very drunken man leaves a New York City bar and hails a taxi. As the cab pulls over, the drunkard motions the driver to open the passenger window. He asks, "Do you have room in here for a case of beer and a pizza? The cabby says, "Sure." The drunk then leans into the window and throws up all over the cab.

"Pick Up Sticks"

TYN – Four Straws (preferably red stirrers – also used in coffee), a bar napkin and some matches.

THE TRICK – To pick up three straws set up in a triangle formation using only one straw.

Step 1: You'll need to set-up the straws. This is done by melting the end of two straws together as shown in Illustration 1.

Illustration 1

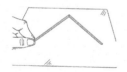

Step 2: Melt the end of the third straw to create an opening / balancing point as shown in Illustration 2.

Illustration 2

Step 3: Now place the three straws on the bar napkin as shown in Illustration 3.

Illustration 3

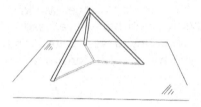

Step 4: Challenge the group to pick up the three straws using only the fourth. Explain the rules:

1. No bending the pick-up straw.
2. No touching the napkin or three straws.
3. You must be able to lift all three.

Step 5: Demonstrate the solution by placing the pick up straw against the two connected straws as shown in Illustration 4.

Illustration 4

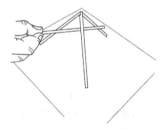

Step 6: Gently push the straws back until the third falls between the two. Now lift the three straws together as shown in Illustration 5.

Illustration 5

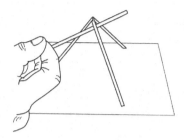

"Pull it Through the Middle"

TYN – Two 2" straws or 2 pen caps or 2 wine corks.

THE TRICK – To place two objects, one in each hand while interlocking fingers seemingly pulling each through the middle.

Step 1: Instruct everyone to place their two corks between their thumb and four fingers as shown in Illustration 1.

Illustration 1

Step 2: Demonstrate the solution and challenge your audience to give it a try. The trick is solved by placing the end of each cork on your opposite thumb as shown in Illustration 2.

Illustration 2

Step 3: Wrap each pointing finger around to touch the other ends of the straws as
Shown in Illustration 3.

Illustration 3

Step 4: Once you have both straws, roll your wrists out to open up your hands to simulate pulling it through the middle as shown in Illustration 4.

Illustration 4

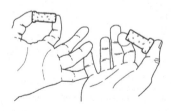

"Bottle Rocket"

TYN – An empty whiskey bottle with just a few drops left in it, a straw, a toothpick and matches.

THE TRICK – Create a bottle rocket from a few simple items you'll find at the bar.

Step 1: Place the toothpick through the straw as shown in Illustration 1.

Illustration 1

Step 2: Pour some hot water from the faucet over the whiskey bottle for a couple of minutes.

Step 3: Place the bottle on the bar, put the straw in the bottle as shown in Illustration 2. Drop a lit match into the bottle and enjoy the fireworks.

Illustration 2

Enhancement: Attach a miniature drink umbrella to the straw for added effect.

Story: The Origin of the Word Whiskey

Where does the word "Whiskey" come from? It is Irish for *water of life*. It describes all liquor distilled from grain, corn is bourbon and barleys are scotch.

CHAPTER 9

WORD/NUMBER TRICKS

"Gray Elephants in Denmark"

TYN (Things You'll Need) – A captive audience with remedial math skills.

THE TRICK – To run through a sequence of math questions. When finished the majority of participants should have "Gray Elephants in Denmark" on their brain.

Step 1: Ask everyone to think of a number between 2 and 9.

Step 2: Multiply that number by nine to get a two digit number.

Step 3: Instruct everyone to add their two digits together to get a single digit number,

Step 4: Take the single digit number and subtract five.

Step 5: Say that if A=1, B=2, C=3 and forth – each person should have a letter that corresponds with their number.

Step 6: Ask everyone to think of a country that begins with that letter.

Step 7: Tell everyone to take the second letter of their country and think of an animal that begins with that letter.

Step 8: Think of a common color of that animal.

Step 9: When everyone is finished you share, "There are No Grey Elephants in Denmark"

Riddle: 53 Bicycles

You're the detective. You're called to investigate a murder in the back room of Joe's Saloon. As you enter the room, you notice the victim slumped in his chair at the card table, surrounded by 53 bicycles. What's the significance of the 53 bicycles and why did the person get killed? **Answer:** Page 93

"The New Math – a.k.a. Dave Math"

TYN – Two bar napkins and a pen.

THE TRICK: Watch your friends "goof up" on simple math.

Step 1: Write down the following numbers on a bar napkin.

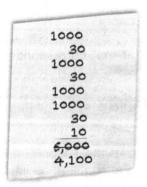

Step 2: Cover the numbers with the other bar napkin and announce to everyone that you'd like for them to add up the following #'s in their head. Tell them you will go as slow as necessary, asking them to say OK to go to the next number.

Step 3: Once you have passed the last 10, ask everyone to share their total. Eight out of 10 people will say 5,000. If everyone in the group answers 5,000, show them the crossed out number and repeat Step #2 until everyone figures out "the New Math."

Riddle: Count

If you were to spell out numbers, how far would you have to go until you would find the letter "A"?
Answer: Page 93

Story: What is Proof?

Proof is a measurement of alcohol content. The simple ratio is 1% equals 2% alcohol proof. Grain or pure alcohol is 200 proof. Beer is traditionally between 8-12% proof or 4-6% alcohol by content.

"Push-Ups"

TYN – At least one willing participant.

THE TRICK: Challenge your friends to a push-up contest.

Step 1: Bet your friend a drink that you can do "between two and three-hundred push-ups in less than a minute." They will assume 200 to 300.

Step 2: Once you've taken the bet, ask your friend to start a 60-second timer.

Step 3: Get into a push-up position and do three or more push-ups to win the bet. You have succeeded in doing between two to 300.

Joke: How many bouncers does it take to screw in a light bulb?

Five. One to screw in the light bulb and four to say, "You're getting H-U-G-E."

CHAPTER 10
UTENSIL TRICKS

"A Nose that Always Knows"

TYN (Things You'll Need) – A regular table or teaspoon.

THE TRICK – To balance a spoon on your nose.

Step 1: Challenge everyone to pick up their spoons and attempt to balance them on their nose.

Step 2: Demonstrate the solution by fogging up (breathing on) the spoon to create condensation. Then place the spoon on your nose. The moisture should help create a bond.

Joke: Did you ever hear that beer makes you smarter? It made Bud Wiser.

Story: The Origin of the Word Pub

Where does the word "Pub" come from? Pub is short for a Public House. Public houses are businesses that serve alcoholic drinks such as beer and ale, and usually also non-alcoholic drinks such as lemonade, coca cola, tea, coffee to be consumed within the limits of the public house. Pubs are found in English-speaking countries such as England, Ireland, Scotland, Canada, and the United States. In villages and small towns in many parts of England, Ireland, and Scotland, pubs are the center of community life. Some pubs hire bands or singers to entertain customers. If the pub has rooms where people can sleep at night, it is usually called an inn.

"A Knife in the Hand"

TYN – One butter / regular table knife per participant. Nothing sharp, definitely not steak knives.

THE TRICK – Challenge everyone to grab their knife and in one swift motion move from Illustration 1 to Illustration 2 without taking their hands off the knife.

Step 1: Instruct everyone to place the knife between their thumb and their hands as shown in Illustration 1.

Illustration 1

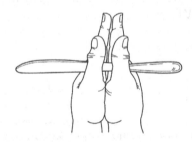

Step 2: Explain that they must go from Illustration 1 to Illustration 2 without taking their hands off the knife. Demonstrate the position of Illustration 2 by taking one hand off of the knife at a time and placing it back on top. Challenge everyone to give it a try.

Illustration 2

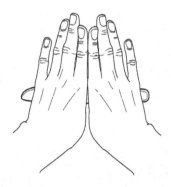

Step 3: After their futile attempts, demonstrate the solution. Hold the knife as shown in Illustration 1 making sure to hold it firmly in your left hand. The ends of knife should be pointing to 9 o'clock and 3 o'clock. The first step is to rotate the knife clockwise so that the tip and end of the knife now face 12 and 6 o'clock as shown in Illustration 3. Continue to rotate your left wrist so that you turn your left palm down towards the floor. Keep your right hand loosely on the knife while sliding your right thumb under your left palm. Place your right fingers over the knife. The end result will have the knife completing a 180-degree turn with your hand now on top of the knife as shown in Illustration 2.

Enhancement: Once the group has solved the trick, challenge them to go from Illustration 2 to Illustration 1 – the reverse move. The key to coming back is placing the right thumb under the knife in the left palm as shown in Illustration 4. Rotate both wrists until you return to a prayer position as shown in Illustration 1.

Illustration 3

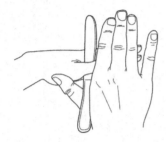

Story: The origin of "Wet your whistle"

Many years ago in England, pub frequenters had a whistle baked into the rim or the handle of their ceramic cups. When they needed a refill, they used the whistle to get some service. "Wet your whistle" is the phrase inspired by this practice.

Joke: Did you hear about the duck that walked into a bar?

After he ordered his beer he said to the bartender, "Just put it on my bill."

CHAPTER 11
TOOTHPICK/MATCH TRICKS

"The Equation"

TYN (Things You'll Need) – 16 matches or toothpicks.

THE TRICK – Setting up toothpicks / matches and moving only one to solve an equation.

Step 1: Set up the following equation shown in Illustration 1.

Illustration 1

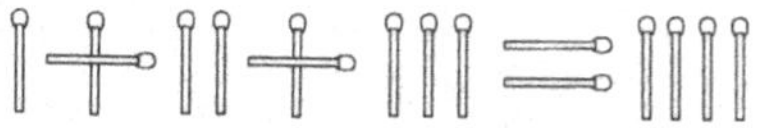

Step 2: Challenge the group to solve the equation by only moving one match and adhering to the following rules:

1. You can only touch the matches on the left hand side of the equation. The equal sign is off limits.
2. The one match you move must also be placed back down on the left side. Let them know that additional +'s and –'s can be made to solve the equation.

Step 3: Demonstrate the solution by moving one match and placing it down to create an additional + sign as shown in Illustration 2.

Illustration 2

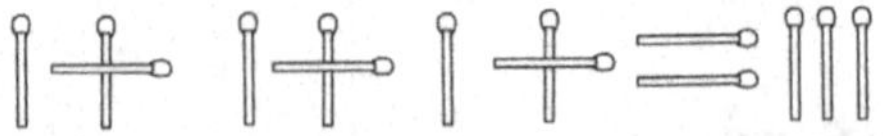

"A Horse is a Horse of Course . . ."

TYN – Five matches or toothpicks.

THE TRICK – To move only one match and be able to re-shape the horse looking in a different direction.

Step 1: Arrange the five matches/toothpicks to resemble a horse as shown in Illustration 1.

Illustration 1

Step 2: Challenge the group to solve the trick after you explain the following rules:

1. You can only move one match and it must be placed back down.
2. After the move, the horse must in the same exact shape and the horse must be looking in a different direction.

Step 3: Solve the equation by moving the back leg and placing it down as shown in Illustration 2.

Illustration 2

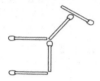

Joke: A three legged dog walks into a bar

He says, "I'm looking for the man who shot my paw."

"The Martini and Olive"

TYN – Four matches / toothpicks and a piece of paper or head of a match (to resemble an olive.)

THE TRICK – To separate the olive from the martini, reforming the glass in two glasses.

Step 1: Set up the martini glass with the four matches / toothpicks as shown in Illustration 1.

Illustration 1

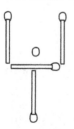

Step 2: Challenge the group to recreate the martini glass in two moves – leaving the untouched olive outside of the glass.

Step 3: To solve the trick, make the two moves as shown in Illustrations 2 and 3.

Illustration 2   **Illustration 3**

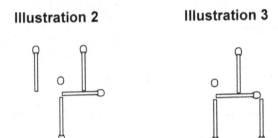

Story: The Origin of the Gibson

Where does the drink Gibson come from? A Gibson is a martini with onions, in place of olives. It comes from an English salesman who did most of his selling while entertaining. His practice was to liquor up his clients while remaining sober himself. No one ever ordered a martini with onions, so with help from the establishment, his customers never knew. He merely drank water with onions.

"4 Equal Triangles"

TYN – Six toothpicks or wooden matches.

THE TRICK – Create four equal triangles with six matches/toothpicks.

Step 1: Place three of the matches in an equal triangle as shown in Illustration 1.

Illustration 1

Step 2: Challenge the group to create three additional equal triangles using the remaining three matches.

Step 3: Solve the trick by making a three dimensional structure as shown Illustration 2.

Illustration 2

Story: Where does gin come from?

Gin comes from the Netherlands, where it is called jenever, also known as genièvre and genever. It's Dutch for juniper. Gin is a clear liquor distilled from grain and flavored with juniper berries. Popular myth holds that it was invented as a blood cleanser by a 17th century chemist. Gin is easy to make because it requires no aging, making it very popular during the prohibition era.

Joke: A giraffe walks into a bar...

He says, "The highballs are on me!!"

"Make a Square"

TYN - Four matches and toothpicks.

THE TRICK – Using the matches and toothpicks in Illustration 1 and then moving one match to create a square.

Step 1: Set up the four matches/toothpicks as shown in Illustration 1.

Illustration 1

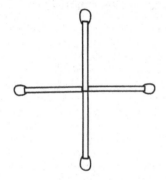

Step 2: Move the top match up a bit in order to create a square as shown in Illustration 2.

Illustration 2

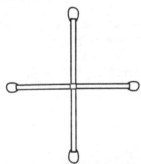

Joke: Jagermeister shots

A young man walks up and sits down at a bar. "What'll you have?" the bartender asks. Six shots of Jagermeister replied the young man. Are you celebrating something inquires the bartender? The young man blushes and whispers: "Yeah, today I had my first BJ." The bartender smiles and shoots back, "Well, in that case, I'll you give you a seventh on the house. The young man thinks quickly and responds: "No offense sir, but if six shots won't get rid of the taste, nothing will."

"Two Boxes out of Nine"

TYN – 24 toothpicks and matches.

THE TRICK – To reduce nine boxes to two by removing eight matches.

Step 1: Place the 24 toothpicks/matches in a tic-tac-toe shape as shown in Illustration 1.

Illustration 1

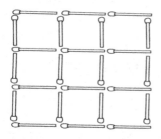

Step 2: Challenge the group to remove eight matches and create two squares. The only rule is that the boxes are not to be touching one another.

Step 3: The solution is to remove the eight matches as shown in Illustration 2.

Illustration 2

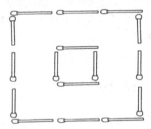

Story: The definition of Cocktail.

From Washington Irving's *Knickerboxers History of New York,* "Cock Tail, then is a stimulating liquor, composed of spirits of any kind, sugar, water and bitters." The etymology of the word is French. A coquetel was a mixed drink introduced in France during the revolution.

"Four out of Five Ain't Bad"

TYN – 16 matches.

THE TRICK – To start with five boxes and move two matches to create four.

Step 1: Arrange the 16 matches to create five boxes as shown in Illustration 1.

Illustration 1

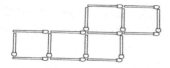

Step 2: Challenge the group to move two matches to create four boxes while adhering to the following rules:

1. The two matches must be placed back down into the puzzle.
2. The four boxes left must be physically touching each other.
3. All four boxes must be identical squares.

Step 3: Solve the trick by moving the two matches as shown in Illustration 2.

Illustration 2

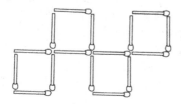

Joke: A bear walks into a bar...

He says to the bartender, "I'll have a..ah.. ahh..ahhh." The bartender replies, "Why such the big paws?"

"Welding Matches"

TYN – A book of wooden matches and a quarter.

THE TRICK – Remove the quarter from under the balanced match without disturbing or touching either of the two matches.

Step 1: Set up the book of matches, quarter and two matches as shown in Illustration 1.

Illustration 1

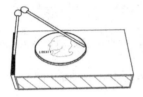

Step 2: Challenge the group to remove the quarter without touching or disturbing the two matches.

Step 3: Solve the trick by lighting the two matches. The heads of the matches will attach and the end of the match on the quarter will curl up and lift away as shown in Illustration 2.

Illustration 2

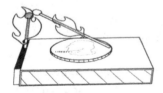

At this point, blow-out the flame and retrieve the quarter. You will have neither touched or disturbed the two matches when you lift the quarter.

Story: The origin of the "Whambulance?"

This term is a great comeback/reply to someone who is constantly complaining or whining. During a bout of complaining, you interject, "What's that I hear in the background. Is that the wha-ambulance?" Do a circular motion with your pointing fingers the air, while you cry out "waaaaah, waaaaah, waaaaah" simulating an ambulance siren.

"The 15 Match Game"

TYN – 15, 19 or 23 matches.

The Trick – To alternate picking between one and three matches from a pile with an opponent and never be left with the last match.

Setup: Count out exactly 15, 19 or 23 matches.

Step 1: Find a willing opponent and make a small bet on the contest.

Step 2: Challenge them to see who will be left with the last match. Explain that during each turn you can take between one and three matches from the pile.

Step 3: You are guaranteed to never lose as you go first. Your first move will always be to take two matches. For example if you start with 15 – the total will now be 13. Whatever your opponent takes – you need to take X number of matches so your total number for both moves equals 4. For example He/She takes 1 and you take 3: He/She takes 2 and you take 2 or He/She takes 3 and you take 1. Repeat this process twice and you will be left 5 matches with it being their turn. Whatever match they take, they are destined to lose as you will leave them with the last match.

Step 4: Your opponent might catch on that they always seem to lose when you go first. Oblige them and let them start the game. The object remains to get to 13 or 9 matches first. If your opponent takes one match as a first move – you simply take one and you've got them at 13. If they take two, you should take one (leaving 12). You would then hope they picked one or two on the next turn – allowing you to pick two or one respectively to get them to 9.

"The Scale Game"

TYN – Nine matches or toothpicks.

THE TRICK – To be able to detect the one match out of nine which is a heavier weight by only using a scale three times.

Step 1: Give the group nine matches and an imaginary scale. Instruct them that they can only using a traditional scale three times. After the third weighing, they must be able to tell which match is the heaviest.

Step 2: Demonstrate the solution by separating the matches into three groups as shown in Illustration 1.

Illustration 1

Step 3: Place the first two groups on either side of the scale. If they are equal, then we can assume the heavy match is in the third group. Otherwise the group which weighs more will contain the heavy match.

Step 4: Take the three matches from the heavy group and place two of its matches on one end of the scale. Place the remaining match from the group plus one match from the other two groups onto the other end. If the two matches from the group weigh more you can deduce that one is the heavy match. Use the scale a third time placing one match on each end. If the remaining match from the group plus the additional match is heavier, then you can deduce that the third match is the heavy match.

Story: Ps & Qs

Where does the saying: "Mind your P's and Q's come from? The P is for Pint and the Q is for Quart, and was commonly abbreviated by the bar staff.

CHAPTER 12
FRUITY TRICKS

"Centrifugal Cherry"

TYN (Things You'll Need) – A brandy snifter, a cherry (no stem) and a pint glass.

THE TRICK – To take an upside down brandy snifter and be able to lift a cherry off the bar and dropping it into a standing glass.

Step 1: Set up the brandy snifter, cherry and pint glass as shown in Illustration 1.

Illustration 1

Step 2: Challenge your group to attempt the trick. Here are the rules:

1. No tilting the snifter, it must stay upside down.
2. You are not allowed to touch the cherry with any part of your body or with any foreign object other than the brandy snifter.

Step 3: After witnessing the futility, demonstrate the solution. This is done by placing the snifter over cherry. Start spinning the glass in a circular motion.

Step 4: Once the cherry spins into the middle of the glass, pick up the glass as you continue to spin in a circulation motion. The centrifugal force will keep the cherry in the glass. Place the brandy snifter over the pint glass and hold it still. Gravity takes effect and the cherry drops into the pint glass.

Enhancements – You can create a hurdle by placing two pint glasses upside down and laying a straw across as shown in Illustration 2. This creates a little added effect.

Illustration 2

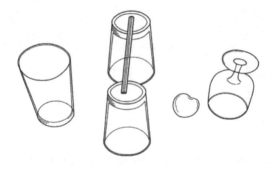

Joke: A guy walks into a bar with a pet alligator...

He puts the alligator up on the bar. He turns to the astonished patrons. "I'll make you a deal. I'll drop my pants, open the mouth of this alligator and place my genitals inside. Then the gator will close his mouth for one minute. He'll then open his mouth and I'll remove my genitals unscathed. In return, each of you will buy me a drink." The crowd murmured their approval. The man stood up on the bar, dropped his trousers and placed his privates in the alligator's open mouth. The gator closed his mouth as the crowd gasped. After exactly one minute, the man grabbed a beer bottle and bashed the alligator on the top of its head. The gator opened his mouth and the man removed his genitals unscathed as promised. The crowd cheered and the first of his free drinks were delivered. The man stood up again and made another offer, "I'll pay anyone one hundred dollars who is willing to give it a try." A hush fell over the crowd. After a while a hand went up in the back of the bar. A woman timidly stood up. "I'll try but you will have to promise not to hit me on the head with the beer bottle."

"All Tied Up in Knots"

TYN – Three or four cherry stems.

THE TRICK – To tie a cherry stem into a knot by utilizing only your tongue.

Step 1: Covertly tie a knot in a cherry and place it discreetly into your mouth.

Step 2: Challenge everyone to attempt to place a stem in their mouths and tie a knot. Believe it or not, this feat can actually be done without trickery. Ninety-eight percent of all people will fail miserably.

Step 3: Demonstrate the solution by placing a cherry stem. Go through the motions as if you are attempting to tie a knot. Tuck the stem into your gums and retrieve the stem you pre-knotted. After 30 seconds or so, pull the knotted stem out of your mouth and display it to the group.

Enhancements – You can pre-pick someone from the group to be your accomplice. Having someone in the group solve the trick lends credibility to the gag. Feel free to make all sorts of innuendo regarding the use of one's tongue and how you found the solution by studying the art of Kama Sutra.

Riddle: Three Lights

There are three light switches in the back room of a bar that turn on three lights in the main bar area. From the back room you cannot see into the main bar. You are given the opportunity to turn the switches on and off as many times as you want but you can only step into the main bar area once. How do you know which switch controls which light bulb? **Answer:** Page 93

"Levitating Orange"

TYN – A linen napkin, an orange and a fork.

THE TRICK – Balance an orange on an outstretched linen napkin.

Step 1: Conceal a fork behind a linen napkin in your right hand as shown Illustration 1.

Illustration 1

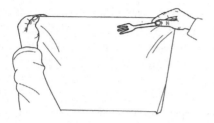

Step 2: Grab an orange with your left hand as you let go of the left side of the napkin. Be sure to keep the fork concealed.

Step 3: As you seemingly try to balance the orange on the edge of the napkin, covertly stick the form in the orange as shown in Illustration 2.

Illustration 2

Step 4: Stretch out the napkin a bit while you bob the orange up and down. You have created the illusion of levitation.

Story: What the origin of Tip or Tips?

In terms of the "gratuity" definition, the word tip most likely comes from a popular form of speech among thieves, beggars and hustlers, called the "Thieves' Cant." The first documented usage of "tip" this way dates back to 1610. At some point within the next century, this sense of the word spread to being used by non-thieves as referring to money given as a bonus for service rendered, with the first documented instance of this definition popping up in 1706 in the George Farquhar play, *The Beaux Stratagem*, "Then I, Sir, tips me the Verger with half a Crown..." **Source:** Today I Found Out

Last Joke: A horse, a giraffe and a bear walk into a bar...

The bartender takes one look at all three and says, "What's this... some kind of joke."

ANSWERS TO RIDDLES

Page 10: "What is It" - answer: Last Name.

Page 21: "Half of all Americans" - answer: Birthplace

Page 21: "Water" - answer: He had hiccups.

Page 23: "Two Identical Twins" - answer: The ice contains poison.

Page 33: "Greater than God" - answer: Nothing.

Page 40: "14th Floor" - answer: He's a midget.

Page 41: "Joe and Fred" - answer: They are goldfish.

Page 49: "Spoiler" - answer: Honey.

Page 52: "Hangman" - answer: He stood on a block of ice.

Page 54: "Three statements" - answer: Coffin

Page 55: "Dead Presidents" - answer: You can't name the President on the ten. Alexander Hamilton was never President. He was the first Secretary of the Treasury.

Page 57: "All 50 States" - answer: Just say, "All 50 States."

Page 66: "53 Bicycles" - answer: Cheating at cards.

Page 67: "Count" - answer: One Thousand.

Page 90: "Three Lights" - answer: Turn the first switch on for two minutes. Then turn it off and switch on the second light switch. Now walk into the main room. The light that's on is the second switch. The warm one is the first one and the room temperature light is the third switch.

"ACK"KNOWLEDGEMENTS & "STAN"DARD THANK YOU'S

We'd like to thank all of the people who gave us advice, inspiration and wisdom, not to mention tricks, riddles, jokes and stories as we were writing the book. This is not a complete list by any means. Mainly because we suffer from a syndrome called CRS (Can't Remember Sh*t.) So if we left you off this list, we owe you a drink the next time out.

Judith (aka - Ima) and the rest of the Ackerman clan... The Whole Phelps family: Mom & Dad, John Jr. and Sandy, Gee and Jim, Mary Ann and Micky, Alice, John III, Laura, Michael, Kevin and Nicole... Carlos and the whole staff at the Blue Moon Mexican Cafe, Stacy Kitch for giving us our first scrapbook/journal... Adam Brett (aka AB or Cherry)... Bo Johnson for the classic "The Nines"... Robyn and Jorge Fuenmayor for all the jokes/riddles via email.... Kenny Merritt... Dave Cota.... Andrea Swick... Patricia Schmidt for "7 & 7, Duh"... Kent Lovett... Jim Cagney's Dad for "The Arb"... Killeen Mullen for "Sugar/Sweet and Low"... Ryan Macaulay (aka RyMac) for "Lime/Corona"... Brian Emmerich... Harry Cocciolo for "Snap, Crackle & Pop"... Cecil Mamiit for "A Rose is a Rose"... Brendan for "Four Equal Triangles"... Gene Keohane... Chris Hall & Rich Silverman... Sam Rothman... Jason Harris... Rich Pastor... Rob Petrucelli... Dan Hull... Jody Frank for "Cheers"... Sal from Senor Swanky's for the "Beer Snorkel"... Mike Briggs for the "Ultimate Wedding Trick"... John Picco for "Snatch"... Kris Leeper... Jeff Hawes... John Cusack for "A Dime for Every Quarter"... Greg Denard... Dave Murphy and Jennie Craig.

ABOUT THE AUTHORS

(Picture taken in 2000)

Stan "The Man" Phelps (pictured left) lives in North Carolina with his wife Jennifer and two boys Thomas and James. Known to possess a huge power draw in golf and worst service toss know to man in the sport of tennis, Stan is the founder of *PurpleGoldfish.com*. He is a keynote speaker and workshop facilitator focused on the future of customer experience and employee engagement. Stan is a Forbes Contributor, IBM Futurist, TEDx Speaker and the author of six books: *Purple Goldfish, Green Goldfish, Golden Goldfish, Blue Goldfish, Red Goldfish* and *Pink Goldfish.*

David "City Champ" Ackerman (pictured right) lives on the Upper West Side of Manhattan where he resides at "Dave-Land." He's known throughout the Big Apple as a mean tennis player and restaurateur. He is currently the General Manager/Owner of the Fat Monk, a Gastropub located on 949 Columbus Ave (between 106 and 107th St.) on the Upper West Side on Manhattan.

EPILOGUE

It took us 19 years to publish this book. Back in the day there was talk of a sequel. We affectionately called it, "Part Deux."

No promises, but do you have a trick, riddle, joke or story that you'd like to submit for the second edition?

Email us at:

stan@purplegoldfish.com or davexyxyxy@yahoo.com

LAGNIAPPE (*a little something extra thrown in for good measure*) – if you ever catch us out at a bar, ask about the "Statue of Liberty." It's one of our all time favorite bar tricks. Like George Burns' last name, it's hot. Add in a little danger and the fact that it needs to be seen to be believed.

Final words. To steal a line from Douglas Adams in the *Hitchhiker's Guide to the Galaxy* series,

> *"So long and thanks for all the fish."*